# PRAY
# WAIT
# STAY

## 31 DAYS OF DECLARATIONS

Revised Edition

# LASHAWN WILSON

**ISBN: 978-1-958404-75-1**

Cover Design by:
Toni-Kay Bromfield

Pray – because we ought always to pray and not lose heart (Luke 18:1 AMP)

Wait – because we gain strength and new power in expectancy (See Isaiah 40:31)

Stay – because even after you received strength after you have prayed and seen the manifestation from your declaration you should remain in His presence and at His feet …… for the fullness of joy and pleasure forever more (See Psalm 16:11 KJV)

Stay – commit your way to the Lord; trust in Him to act. He will bring forth your righteousness as the light and your justice as the noonday (See Psalm 37:4 KJV)

# Acknowledgments

My first and extraordinary debt of gratitude goes to the Holy Spirit, for inspiring me to write this book. It is through His leadership and guidance, from start to finish, line upon line, and for every revelation of Scripture that this body of work could be completed. I credit all that and more to the Holy Spirit who dwells in me and instructs me in His truth.

I thank my editor, Mrs. Zelia Gibson-Brown, who has worked tirelessly with me to see the completion of this book. I have learned so much from you on this journey and I thank you for every lesson. Thank you for giving me an attainable deadline to ensure that the book was completed. I thank God for the grace He has given you to provide constructive criticism. You have always believed in me and every instruction I have received from the Lord. I thank you for trusting the God in me and assisting me on the journey however you could.

To Ms. Toni-Kay Bromfield, I thank you for being there - for everything. You are a "Jill of all trades" and I thank God for this gift He has given you. I remember one day I was stuck on writing, and you provided a solution to get me back on track, and indeed it worked. You have been an integral part of my journey, and like Zelia, you run with every assignment the Lord instructs me on. I thank you for creating the cover art for this book. Every time the Lord gives me a vision, I never usually have to tell you what I want, you seek the Lord for yourself to know what graphic artwork goes well with the vision the Lord has given me, and I have never second guessed you nor have I been disappointed in what you illustrate. I trust the gift God has given you and I bless God for you and this gift.

To Bishop O'mar Wedderburn, I thank you for your time and your teachings in the Word. You are a wealth of biblical revelation, and it is a great wonder to behold. Thank you for reading through the book and providing critical insights. I appreciate you as a father and a friend.

Lastly, I would like to thank Pastor/Prophet Tevaun Brown for starting the 61 Days of Midnight Prayer (Qavah) on his church's Zoom platform. It was during midnight prayer that the Lord instructed me to write this book. I thank God for your obedience to this avenue to pray.

# Foreword

In light of new age teachings creeping into the church, much of the church's affirmations are laced with new age beliefs. I am skeptical about books that encourage declaration, particularly those not rooted in sound doctrine but instead permeate the shenanigans of the law of attraction. The idea that one's thoughts can control the world around them and conjure their desires is frightening and unbiblical.

No Christian is given authority to impose their desires — instead, they are required to proclaim the promises of God. Christians are given authority only to pronounce what the Lord has decreed — this is not a call for God to respond to the saints' wishes, but for the saints to respond to God's will according to Psalm 2:7 KJV "I will declare the decree the LORD hath said unto me..."

In this book, Ms. Wilson clarifies what she means by declaration and thoroughly explains the biblical position of what it is. I applaud Ms. Wilson for announcing her intention to write 31 Days of Declaration for her readers to rightly declare the promises of God for His children, instead of misguided declarations —

if not aligned with the Word of God, it is incorrect.

Promised scriptures released over God's people throughout the Old and New Testaments reinforce each chapter in her book. Ms. Wilson has eloquently applied these assurances to the believers' daily lives. I particularly like the book's structure — there is a declaration every day of the month, alongside anecdotal experiences of Ms. Wilson. Her writing style should keep her readers engaged, as this book is easy to read, relatable, relevant, and real. Her readers will enjoy perusing the one-month declarations and, perhaps, beg her to write a follow-up quickly.

Overall, 31 Days of Declaration is a good and coherent book that reads like a daily meditation with God's assurance to shift any circumstances affecting the Christians' lives.

Why wait? Get your copy and declare the Word over your life now!

**Bishop O'mar Wedderburn**
**Author**

# Endorsements

This book of declarations is indeed an inspired work of the Holy Spirit. As I read each day, I am struck with the simplicity yet powerful nature of the words being declared. The writer pulls me to acknowledge the smallness of the enemy, contrasted with the greatness of my God, and in so doing she liberates my mind and speech to boldly declare what God has already said about me. I appreciate the fact that there is no attempt to conjure up some new decrees to satisfy personal ambitions, but rather just a simple, yet profound acknowledgment of the Word of the Spirit. This is a relevant and much-needed book of declarations, and I am excited to see the impact it will make.

**Pastor Rachael Thompson**
**Fellowship Tabernacle**

***

I have known Lashawn Wilson for a few years – she has shared with Perpetual Sounds of Praise as a dedicated member – always able to "bring the fire." Her ability to shift atmospheres in worship and obvious commitment to carrying the banner of Christ high is always evident.

She has seen some rough days, but I always remind her – "Keep your heart pure" ...and she aims to do just that. For how can we offer unto our Lord a sacrifice of praise, yet our hearts are not pure before Him?

Fast forward to Day 4 where her declaration is based on Psalm 66:18 where the Lord reminds us not to regard iniquity in our hearts. Believe me when I say that it was Lashawn's obedience and surrender to Christ that drove her to have what you hold in your hands - A book of declarations and prayers. She may be down, but she is not out. We can glean so much from these declarations and with a greater understanding of who we are in Christ and the spirit realm – *we will win – we will never lose.*

May your journey through these declarations find you growing in the knowledge and grace of Christ. Get ready to go deep – give your all for the turnaround. I know you will be lifted.

**Dr. Nadine Blair**
**Author and Radio Personality**

# Contents

# A Message for You

This book was God-breathed after my encounter with the Lord during midnight prayer. He assigned me to release 31 days of daily declarations, by the decrees of the Lord, for an alignment of His people over their new year.

The New Year I speak of is not based on the Gregorian Calendar, but the one based on the instruction the Lord gave to Moses and Aaron in The Book of Exodus. "The LORD said to Moses and Aaron in the land of Egypt, "This month shall be the beginning of months to you; it is to be the first month of the year to you." Exodus 12:1-2 (AMP)

The beginning month of the New Year is called Abib/Nisan. This is the first month of the Ancient Hebrew calendar which usually begins the middle of March to the middle of April.

Before one of these declarations is made, it is vital that we accurately define what a declaration is, how essential declarations are, and what it means to make a decree.

According to the Merriam-Webster dictionary, to declare is to make known formally, officially, or explicitly. In essence, to declare is to state (out loud) a fact. On the other hand, the word decree, per the dictionary, is an order usually having the force of law or a religious ordinance enacted by a council or titular head. Simply put, a decree is to issue an authoritative command.

Based on biblical principles, the decrees of God are His will, purpose, and plans, how He deals with us, and what He has already told us will happen. The decrees of God are coherent with His character, which is of justice, knowledge, immutability, and goodness. Therefore, when we declare, we restate a law already set. *We, therefore, cannot declare something that God has not sanctioned.*

It is very important to declare God's Word because it builds your faith in Him. There are some practical benefits to "decreeing a thing". Don Stewart (2007) of the Blue Letter Bible gives some great examples: we gain confidence in God, it provides hope, and makes us humble.

The Scriptures contain several general statements about the decrees of God. Let us look at a few examples that show these decrees.

In the book of Isaiah, Chapter 14:26-27, the Amplified Version reads,

*"This is the plan [of God] decided for the whole earth [regarded as conquered and put under tribute by Assyria], and this is the hand [of God] that is stretched out over all the nations. The Lord of hosts has decided and planned, and who can annul it? His hand is stretched out, and who can turn it back?"*

In this, we see a brief prophecy against the Assyrians living in Isaiah's time. The Lord openly declares His purpose to break the Assyrians in His land. It shows that God never has to adjust His plans for the world or anyone.

In Ephesians Chapter 1:11 (AMP), Paul wrote, "In Him also we have received an inheritance [a destiny—God claimed us as His own], having been predestined (chosen, appointed beforehand) according to the purpose of Him who works everything in agreement with the counsel *and* design of His will." This teaches us that the decrees of the Lord have long gone out before us.

Believers, it is routine at the beginning of the year for people to have New Year's resolutions, but what about New Year's declarations? We get up and command our morning and our week, so how about we set the tone for our year? Let's discuss how we want our days, weeks, and months to be. Let this be our mood board to blueprint the revelation given to us by the Lord for how our year ought to be. Let these declarations set the tone and meet us in the future after we have prayed, declared, and sought after the Lord.

I pray that for every word declared and every page written, God will cause these declarations to meet you in your future so you may come back to what you have said and write your testimony of that day when you see it come to pass.

A few pages have been placed at the end for you to document your own experience and keep a record of your encounters throughout these past 31 days.

Everything written is in the Name of Jesus Christ and His authority and through His power.

The purpose of this book is not for you to utter wild declarations but to declare the Will of God, which is the Word of God.

The effectual fervent prayer of a righteous
man availeth much.

- James 5:16 KJV

# PRAY
# WAIT
# STAY

## 31 DAYS OF DECLARATIONS

# Day 1
# A New Year of Thanksgiving

---

L ord, I thank You. This is the year You have made; I will rejoice and be glad in it (Psalm 118:24, AMP). Today, I want to thank You. I enter this year with thanksgiving in my heart and into Your courts with praise (Psalm 100:4, AMP).

Father, I declare I will be more thankful unto You this year. I repent for every time that I was not thankful before as I begin this time of prayer and declarations, and I ask that You forgive me for every time I was not thankful enough.

I declare that I will have a song in my heart, in the good times and bad, to praise You despite the season I am in. I declare that out of my belly will flow rivers of gratefulness. I declare that I will thank You in the morning, and I will thank You before I lay my head to rest at night. I declare that Thanksgiving will come to my home this year. I declare that Thanksgiving will be spewed out of my family and that we will be known for being thankful. Father, Your Word says that everything with breath should praise You, so I declare thankfulness out of the generations that will come after me.

I declare this is the year I will be more thankful than I complain and grateful than grumpy in Jesus' Name. Amen

# Day 2
## Continued Thanks

Father, I am still in awe of how You kept me throughout last year and spared my life to live to see another. I am eternally grateful for Your love and kindness toward me. Indeed, I am undeserving of Your blessings, care, and favour, so I thank You for this love.

I thank You, Lord, for keeping my mind at peace and staying on You. For the times when my mind shifted, God, I repent.

Today, I declare that I will thank You for Your goodness. Your steadfast love endures forever. (1 Chronicles 16:34, AMP)

I declare that I will always be thankful for the strength of God. That strength that is like no other - that omnipotent strength. Father, I declare that I, in thanksgiving, will remember that You are my strength and that in Your hands are power and might, to make prominent and give strength to all as stated by Your word. (1 Chronicles 29:12-13, AMP).

I will praise You, oh God, and I will magnify You with thanksgiving. (Psalm 69:30, KJV).

I declare that this year, my mouth will not be shut up, but I will make a joyful noise to You, who is the rock of my salvation, and I will always come before Your presence with a song of thanksgiving. I declare that I will shout joyfully to You with songs. (Psalm 95:1-2, AMP)

In the Name of Jesus, I declare that I will be thankful not just this year but forever. Just as You rejoice over me with song (Zephaniah 3:17, AMP), so too will I rejoice.

I will rejoice in hope - the hope of salvation - until You come. In Jesus' Name. Amen.

# Day 3
## Consistency in Prayer

---

I discovered the story of an ex-satanist named James Kawalya on YouTube. He spoke on the importance of praying as a child of God and what covenant prayers do to the kingdom of darkness. He testified that he was explicitly assigned to take down people in ministry, who live consecrated lives, and those with powerful prayer ministries. What stood out to me profoundly was when he went into how he was assigned to break a covenant prayer a Pastor was on, because if the Pastor had fulfilled the timeline he set out to accomplish, it would cause satanic activity in the region to cease for 70 years.

**Believers, our prayer lives are so important.** Men ought always to pray and not faint (Luke 18:1, KJV).

We sometimes need someone to hold us accountable, so I am placing a calendar in this book to track the days of prayer. You can go back at the end of the year and check your consistency.

I pray it will be an encouragement to you. Let's pray.

## -Declarations-

Father, today I declare that I will pray more for this new year!

I declare, God Almighty, in the power of Your might, that I, _____ (insert name), will pray more. I will obey Your decree to pray without ceasing (1 Thessalonians 5:16, KJV).

I will be persistent and devoted in prayer. I will be alert, focused, and thankful in Jesus' Name. (Colossians 4:2, AMP)

I declare that I will rejoice in hope, be patient in tribulations, and continue steadfastly in prayer. (Romans 12:12, AMP)

I declare that nothing will be able to get between me and my time of prayer with the Lord this year. I, therefore, rebuke every spirit of distraction in the name of Jesus.

I will create a set time to meet with the Lord. I will pray _____ (place set time here). I vow that this is the time I will meet with the Father for this year, and through the help of the Holy Spirit, I will not break this covenant. According to Your Word, if I obey Your voice and keep my covenant, I shall be Your treasured possession among all peoples (Exodus 19:5, AMP).

I declare that I will keep this covenant to pray. In Jesus' Name. Amen.

# 2021 PRAYER CALENDAR

## JANUARY

| M | T | W | T | F | S | S |
|---|---|---|---|---|---|---|
| 1 | 2 | 3 | 4 | 5 | 6 | 7 |
| 8 | 9 | 10 | 11 | 12 | 13 | 14 |
| 15 | 16 | 17 | 18 | 19 | 20 | 21 |
| 22 | 23 | 24 | 25 | 26 | 27 | 28 |
| 29 | 30 | 31 | | | | |

## FEBRUARY

| M | T | W | T | F | S | S |
|---|---|---|---|---|---|---|
| | | | 1 | 2 | 3 | 4 |
| 5 | 6 | 7 | 8 | 9 | 10 | 11 |
| 12 | 13 | 14 | 15 | 16 | 17 | 18 |
| 19 | 20 | 21 | 22 | 23 | 24 | 25 |
| 26 | 27 | 28 | 29 | | | |

## MARCH

| M | T | W | T | F | S | S |
|---|---|---|---|---|---|---|
| | | | | 1 | 2 | 3 |
| 4 | 5 | 6 | 7 | 8 | 9 | 10 |
| 11 | 12 | 13 | 14 | 15 | 16 | 17 |
| 18 | 19 | 20 | 21 | 22 | 23 | 24 |
| 25 | 26 | 27 | 28 | 29 | 30 | 31 |

## APRIL

| M | T | W | T | F | S | S |
|---|---|---|---|---|---|---|
| 1 | 2 | 3 | 4 | 5 | 6 | 7 |
| 8 | 9 | 10 | 11 | 12 | 13 | 14 |
| 15 | 16 | 17 | 18 | 19 | 20 | 21 |
| 22 | 23 | 24 | 25 | 26 | 27 | 28 |
| 29 | 30 | | | | | |

## MAY

| M | T | W | T | F | S | S |
|---|---|---|---|---|---|---|
| | | 1 | 2 | 3 | 4 | 5 |
| 6 | 7 | 8 | 9 | 10 | 11 | 12 |
| 13 | 14 | 15 | 16 | 17 | 18 | 19 |
| 20 | 21 | 22 | 23 | 24 | 25 | 26 |
| 27 | 28 | 29 | 30 | 31 | | |

## JUNE

| M | T | W | T | F | S | S |
|---|---|---|---|---|---|---|
| | | | | | 1 | 2 |
| 3 | 4 | 5 | 6 | 7 | 8 | 9 |
| 10 | 11 | 12 | 13 | 14 | 15 | 16 |
| 17 | 18 | 19 | 20 | 21 | 22 | 23 |
| 24 | 25 | 26 | 27 | 28 | 29 | 30 |

## JULY

| M | T | W | T | F | S | S |
|---|---|---|---|---|---|---|
| 1 | 2 | 3 | 4 | 5 | 6 | 7 |
| 8 | 9 | 10 | 11 | 12 | 13 | 14 |
| 15 | 16 | 17 | 18 | 19 | 20 | 21 |
| 22 | 23 | 24 | 25 | 26 | 27 | 28 |
| 29 | 30 | 31 | | | | |

## AUGUST

| M | T | W | T | F | S | S |
|---|---|---|---|---|---|---|
| | | | 1 | 2 | 3 | 4 |
| 5 | 6 | 7 | 8 | 9 | 10 | 11 |
| 12 | 13 | 14 | 15 | 16 | 17 | 18 |
| 19 | 20 | 21 | 22 | 23 | 24 | 25 |
| 26 | 27 | 28 | 29 | 30 | 31 | |

## SEPTEMBER

| M | T | W | T | F | S | S |
|---|---|---|---|---|---|---|
| | | | | | | 1 |
| 2 | 3 | 4 | 5 | 6 | 7 | 8 |
| 9 | 10 | 11 | 12 | 13 | 14 | 15 |
| 16 | 17 | 18 | 19 | 20 | 21 | 22 |
| 23/30 | 24 | 25 | 26 | 27 | 28 | 29 |

## OCTOBER

| M | T | W | T | F | S | S |
|---|---|---|---|---|---|---|
| | 1 | 2 | 3 | 4 | 5 | 6 |
| 7 | 8 | 9 | 10 | 11 | 12 | 13 |
| 14 | 15 | 16 | 17 | 18 | 19 | 20 |
| 21 | 22 | 23 | 24 | 25 | 26 | 27 |
| 28 | 29 | 30 | 31 | | | |

## NOVEMBER

| M | T | W | T | F | S | S |
|---|---|---|---|---|---|---|
| | | | | 1 | 2 | 3 |
| 4 | 5 | 6 | 7 | 8 | 9 | 10 |
| 11 | 12 | 13 | 14 | 15 | 16 | 17 |
| 18 | 19 | 20 | 21 | 22 | 23 | 24 |
| 25 | 26 | 27 | 28 | 29 | 30 | |

## DECEMBER

| M | T | W | T | F | S | S |
|---|---|---|---|---|---|---|
| | | | | | | 1 |
| 2 | 3 | 4 | 5 | 6 | 7 | 8 |
| 9 | 10 | 11 | 12 | 13 | 14 | 15 |
| 16 | 17 | 18 | 19 | 20 | 21 | 22 |
| 23/30 | 24/31 | 25 | 26 | 27 | 28 | 29 |

# Day 4
# Repentance

F ather, You said if I regard iniquity in my heart when I pray, You will not hear me. (Psalm 66:18, KJV) So, Father, right now I pray concerning all acts of iniquity that are offensive to You. I repent for any form of iniquity that is in my heart. I repent for sins known and unknown. I repent for the dirtiness that lives in me from engaging in sin by transgressing Your law.

I declare that this is the year I will call out sin quickly, repent, and remain steadfast in prayer. I declare that no sin of the past years, dating back from even the third or fourth generation, will be able to hinder my prayers going forth and meeting me in the future. I, therefore, repent on behalf of my ancestors. The sins of witchcraft, deception, lust, sexual immorality, lies, and slothfulness, Lord, I call them out now, and I repent. These sins will not hinder my prayer life nor block my prayers from being answered, in Jesus' Name.

I declare that You forget all the sins of my past. I declare I am washed and stepping out in the newness of Christ - the newness in You that has called me with Your lovingkindness and has set me free.

I declare more grace to me in Jesus' Name. Amen.

# Day 5
## Grace and Favour

---

Biblically, the number 5 symbolizes God's grace, goodness, and favour. I do not think it is random that as I wrote the declarations for this day and looked at the time, it was 3:45 am, and as I looked at my phone, it was at 95%.

So, today, we are praying declarations for more of God's grace and favour for this New Year.

## -Declarations-

Father, today I declare according to Your Words in Psalm 5:12 that I am righteous, and because I am righteous, You, oh Lord, have surrounded me with favour as a shield. I thank You, God, that favour surrounds me as a shield. I declare that God's favour is over my life in this New Year in Jesus' Name. There is favour with men and women, favour on the job, which is miraculous and will cause a mind-blowing testimony.

I declare that I walk in, and my steps are aligned with favour. Favour is imprinted upon my life like the Blood of Jesus, and my name is laced and smeared with favour. I declare that when my name is uttered in rooms, it is followed by favour. I declare that favour will overtake my life in Jesus' Name like never before.

God, I also thank You for abundant grace in my life. You said in Your Word that You can make all grace abound to me so that always having all sufficiency in all things, I may abound in every good work (2 Corinthians 9:8, KJV). By this, I thank You for Your grace that abounds. This grace has been sufficient to keep me.

Lord, I thank You for it. In Jesus' Name. Amen.

# Day 6
## Doors of Opportunity

---

Father, You are He who is holy, who is trustworthy, who has the key of David, who opens doors and no one will shut, and who shuts doors and no one opens (Revelations 3:7-8, KJV), and it is in Your Name that I pray today.

Father, today I declare that doors of opportunities are opened for me for this New Year. I pray and declare that every door of lack and scarcity that have followed me in previous years is now shut behind me, never to be reopened in the MIGHTY Name of Jesus. I am now walking through doors of abundance, fruitfulness, and prosperity.

I use my hand prophetically to knock on doors in the realm of the spirit and command every door that has been shut by the enemy in years past to be opened. As I knock by force, I command all doors to my prosperity to be opened now.

I declare that all doors to my freedom will be unlocked now. Doors to financial freedom, mental and physical freedom, freedom over my health, my family, and my educational advancement, I declare that they are unlocked now in the Name of Jesus.

It is so and shall not be otherwise in Jesus' Name. Amen.

# Day 7
# Breaking Down Walls

---

Father, today, I pray concerning walls. I declare every wall placed before me by the enemy to be broken down by the sledgehammer of the Almighty God now!

As I identify you by name, I declare that the sound of my voice breaks you down. Walls of oppression, walls that block my blessing, breakthrough, and deliverance, be broken down now in Jesus' Name. I command walls that are erected before me, to imprison my life and destiny, will crumble by the sound of my voice.

As I walk prophetically, I sound a trumpet in the realm of the spirit, and I declare a shout as the children of Israel did. As I shout, I declare that you, Jericho Wall, are coming down (Joshua 6:5, AMP). The wall of the city blocking my inheritance will fall, and I will go straight ahead in Jesus' Name.

As I utter the decree of Genesis 24:56, I state aloud that I will not be hindered, for the Lord has prospered my way.

It is so and shall not be otherwise in Jesus' Name. Amen.

# Day 8
# The Sound Mind

Father, today, I come before You and pray concerning my mind. I declare that I have the mind of Christ according to Philippians 2:5.

You said in Your Word that to be carnally minded is death (Romans 8:6, KJV), so I rebuke carnality from my mind. I declare that I am spiritually minded and have life and peace because of this. You said You will keep my mind at peace once my mind is stayed on You (Isaiah 26:3, KJV). I declare aloud that my mind is fixed on You now and forever more.

I resist the spirit of fear and declare that I have a sound mind in Jesus' Name; as this is the mind Your Spirit has given me. (2 Timothy 1:7, KJV)

I declare that I am wise. I have the wisdom of the Lord. I declare that the wisdom placed on King Solomon in 1 Kings 4:29 is also on me, as I am of the lineage of Christ.

As I am prophetically armoured with the armour of God, I declare, as was instructed, that I wear the Helmet of Salvation. This helmet is fitted with thoughts of humility. I declare that my affections are set on the things above, not things of the earth. (Colossians 3:2, AMP)

I declare that I will be sober and vigilant (1 Peter 5:8, KJV) in my ways and thoughts.

I declare today that I will think about the things that are true, honest, just, pure, lovely and that are of an excellent report. (Philippians 4:8, KJV).

It is in Jesus' Name that I pray. Amen.

# Day 9
## The Sound Mind

---

The mind is a powerful tool; if the enemy can take control of your mind, he can take control of your life. Dr Nadine Blair wrote a song called 'Pour It Out' with a powerful line I love. It says, "Won't let the whispers of the enemy be louder than God's Word in me". I particularly love that line because it encapsulates how little the enemy's voice is and how big we make it out to be.

Today, I pray to defeat that little voice wholly. I bring every thought into captivity to Christ's obedience in Jesus' Name. (2 Corinthians 10:5, AMP)

### -Declarations-

Father, today I continue the declarations concerning the mind. You said in Your Word that a double-minded man is unstable in all his ways (James 1:8, AMP). I declare that my mind is sound and stable. I follow the decree to put off the old man's corrupt conversations, and I declare that I am renewed in the spirit of my mind. I will put on the new man, who after God, is created in righteousness and true holiness (Ephesians 4:22-24, KJV) in Jesus' Name.

Lord, I thank You that, according to Your Word, You are opening my mind to new mysteries and showing me great and mighty things that I had no prior knowledge of (Jeremiah 33:3, AMP).

Lord, I declare that all imaginations are cast down and brought low, and every high thing that exalts itself against the knowledge of God will be made desolate in Jesus' mighty Name. Amen.

# Day 10
## The Eyes to See

Father, today, as I pray concerning my eyes, I thank You for Your vision. As I thank You for vision, I also want to thank You for what, by faith, I cannot see. I thank You for giving me the faith which is the evidence of the things not seen (Hebrews 11:1, KJV). On the topic of eyes, I thank You that eyes have not seen, nor ears heard, neither has it entered the heart of men what You will do concerning my life because of these daily declarations (1 Corinthians 2:9, AMP).

I now declare that my eyes are open so that I may see the goodness of the Lord in the land of the living (Psalm 27:13, AMP).

I declare that I will guard my eyes and what I put before them. I will also keep my eye-gates pure, so nothing seeps into my heart through them. Through my vision, I will receive clarity on things to do and what not to do. As I see in the physical, I can see more profound things in the spirit realm. And now, Lord, I declare that my spiritual eyes will be opened, and my sight unlocked to a new dimension in You.

I declare a spiritual 20/20 vision laced with clarity and precision this season and beyond in Jesus' Name. Amen.

# Day 11
# The Mouth That Speaks

Father, today, as I come before You, I pray concerning my mouth and voice. Hallelujah! I declare that I will, according to 1 Peter 3:10, keep my tongue free from evil and my lips from speaking guile. Right now, I repent for every ungodly speech or word I have ever uttered from my mouth. I repent for misrepresenting You with my tongue and gossiping (knowingly or unknowingly) in times past, and I ask that You forgive me. Let not my mouth be what blocks my blessings and creates distance between me and You.

I align myself with the words from the Scripture in Ephesians 4:29, and I declare that no unwholesome talk shall come out of my mouth. I declare that I will speak only what helps build others up according to their needs.

I declare that now and forever, my conversations will always be full of grace, seasoned with salt, so I may know how to answer every man (Colossians 4:6, AMP).

Lord, I declare that my voice will carry a sound of wisdom. The frequency of my vocal cords will know each decibel. God, I agree with Your Word in the book of Proverbs 15:28 that the heart of the righteous weighs its answers. Today, I declare that I will weigh every word before I release them out of my mouth. I declare that I speak with wisdom, that faithful instructions are on my tongue (Proverbs 31:26, AMP), and that I will be quick to listen and slow to speak in Jesus' Name (See James 1:19).

Father, I ask that You set a guard over my mouth and keep watch over the door of my lips. (Psalm 141:3, AMP)

I pray by Psalm 119:171-172, may my lips overflow with praise, for You teach me Your decrees.

May my tongue sing of Your Word, for all Your commands are righteous. Thank You, Lord.

Let the words of my mouth, and the meditation of my heart, be acceptable in Your sight, O Lord, my Strength, and my Redeemer (Psalm 19:14, KJV).

It is in Jesus' Name that I pray. Amen.

# Day 12
# The Heart Matters

Father, as I prayed yesterday about my mouth, today, I pray concerning my heart. You said in Your Word, in Matthew 12:34, that out of the abundance of the heart, the mouth speaks. You also said in Proverbs 4:23 that I should guard my heart, for everything I do flows from it.

I pray for a heart like Yours, Lord. All bitterness, wrath, anger, clamour, and evil speaking be put away from me as is in Ephesians 4:31. I pray that animosity, resentment, strife, and fault-finding be eradicated from my life. Let kindness, compassion, and understanding overtake me now. Let the forgiving heart of God be within me. Just as Christ has forgiven me, I will also forgive freely in Jesus' Name.

Father, You said in 1 Corinthians 13:13 that faith, hope, and love abide, but love is the greatest of the three. I declare that love reigns within my heart, and that all that I do, per 1 Corinthians 16:14, be done in love - love, according to 1 Corinthians 13:4-7, that is patient and kind. The love that does not envy or boast. Love that is not arrogant or rude. The love that keeps no record of wrongdoing, that covers a multitude of sins, as 1 Peter 4:8 says. The love that hopes and endures all things.

Let this love, Father, be the love within my heart, now and forever more. In Jesus' Name, Amen.

# Day 13
## Strengthened Faith

I will use this opportunity to be transparent and say that while writing this book, I needed to figure out what I was getting myself into. I have never done so many back-to-back declarations, which has stretched me. I heard God saying, "Write the book," and I obeyed. I did not know what to expect. I just prayed, listened, and, by faith, started to write. We are on the 13th day, and I heard the Lord say, "Talk about faith and make some faith declarations." Again, by faith, we are going to make some declarations. By the time we finish these 31 days, results should already be evident from the declarations. There should already be testimonies of the goodness of God through these declarations. So, let us strengthen faith a bit where faith may be lacking.

You are not reading this book by chance. By faith, you saw the need to get this book and to make these declarations. Let us "sweeten the pot" by releasing faith-strengthening declarations for these next few days.

## -Declarations-

Father, today I pray, as I declare these Scriptures of faith, that my faith is being strengthened with every word. Lord, help me daily to have a little more faith. Help me to stand on Your Word by faith. Help me disregard what I see naturally and focus on what You promised - the things not seen. Help me to operate on a heavenly frequency and timeline of faith. As I go into these declarations, I pray that every seed of doubt planted by the enemy is uprooted now! Lord, I repent for faithlessness, worry, and mistrust in You. Let every seed not planted by my Father be uprooted in the mighty Name of Jesus. Hallelujah!

According to Matthew 21:22, I declare that everything I ask for in prayer, according to my faith, I will, I must receive, and I have received. According to Luke 1:37, nothing is impossible with the Lord. I stand on the conviction that faith is the evidence of things not seen, according to Hebrews 11:1. In the same book of Hebrews, chapter 11, the Word of the Lord says without faith, it is impossible to please God and that whoever draws near to God must believe that He is a Rewarder of those who seek Him. Today, I rise by faith from slumber to seek You, Lord. I know if I stay in Your presence and dwell with You, You will reward me.

Lord, I will pray, wait, and stay because I know my reward is sure, in Jesus' Name. Amen.

# Day 14
## Steps of Faith

I host a yearly event called the Weeping, Wailing, Worshiping Women's Conference. Hosting the last staging in 2019 was a real test of my faith. Before that year, I wrote to sponsors requesting donations - whether monetary, kind, or gifts, but in 2019, the Lord told me to use my savings. Yes, you read that right. Did I think it would take up my entire savings? No. As it turned out, it went way over that, and I did not know how some things for the event would have been paid for.

Let me be transparent again. I am a person who likes to know how the I's will be dotted and how the T's will be crossed. I do not like to go into anything blindly. However, I knew what God said and that I needed to trust Him. Therefore, I decided that although I could not see how, I knew I heard Him, and He would make a way. When the day of the event finally came, all expenses were covered before the event was even over. Hallelujah! One thing God did during the process that completely blew my mind was to cause me to run into someone of prominence, whom I hadn't seen in years, as I casually walked on the road one day. That individual went on to bless my ministry. As we often say in colloquial terms, "Who could it be but God?" That blessing took care of a considerable expense. To this day, I still hear members of the planning committee using that faith moment as a reference to what helped to strengthen their faith. It is my prayer that the faith you have will strengthen the faith of those around you in Jesus' Name. Believers, let us continue to make some declarations of faith today.

## -Declarations-

Father, today I rise; as I walk, I take steps of faith. Your Word says in 2 Corinthians 5:7 to walk by faith, not sight. I declare today that I am doing just that. From this day forth, all my steps are steps of faith and hope. According to Proverbs 3:5-6, I will trust in You with all my heart. Lord, my understanding is futile. I declare that I will not lean on it but acknowledge You in each step, for You are the Director of my path. Hallelujah!

Father, I declare that no longer will I doubt in my heart that You will do what You said. In James 1:5-8, Lord, You spoke of the double-minded man. I rebuke double mindedness from me now. I declare that I will take You at Your Word. I declare I will not be like the waves dashed by the winds, but I am stable in all my ways. I declare that I have consistency in faith in Jesus' Name.

I declare that I, by faith, will say to the mountains, "Be thou moved!" and they will move, according to Matthew 17:20. By faith, I will call things that are out of alignment, into divine alignment by the Will of God. In Jesus' Name. Hallelujah!

I declare that it is by faith that I live and by faith that I breathe. It is by faith that I understand and navigate my day-to-day living. I declare that I spend by the currency of faith and speak a faith-filled vocabulary.

I declare, according to Romans 1:17, that I am the righteousness of God. Therefore, for this cause, I live by faith in Jesus' Name. Amen.

# Day 15
# Unwavering Faith

***

You have made it to the halfway mark, and again, I will be transparent with you. After writing day 13 on faith, my faith began to take a downturn. There was so much that started to happen as I chose to make the declarations of faith. I was down to my last $50JMD, and the gas in my car was almost on 'E' while writing. My faith was being tested. In addition, I came home with limited food resources and went a few days without eating. A good friend of mine brought me some malt beverages and powdered milk, which kept me going.

My focus began to shift as I wrote, and I started to allow the whispers of the enemy to get loud. It is a good thing that I know some Scriptures. I started to tell myself that man shall not live by bread alone (Matthew 4:3-4) and found comfort in that.

There is so much that I have experienced and continue to experience on the journey of writing this book that would make my faith want to waver. I must, however, keep my eyes, ears, and heart fixed on Jesus. The Word says in Philippians 3:14 KJV, I press toward the mark for the prize of God's high calling in Christ Jesus. I, by faith, will continue this journey of faith that will ultimately lead to eternal life.

Will you continue to make these faith steps with me? Let us make some more declarations of faith today. I applaud your consistency. You are halfway through the book.

## -Declarations-

Father, today I thank You that my faith is being strengthened. I stand fully convinced, under Romans 4:20-21, that You can do everything You have promised. I thank You that 2 Timothy 4:7 explains that if I stand in faith, You will be with me throughout my life, especially when I need You most. Lord, thank You for being a guide. Thank You that faith now lives where doubt once occupied. I declare that my name is now changed to Child of Faith and that my testimony will be that of faith. I will walk on by faith throughout this year and the rest of my journey. I declare that my work will be a prelude to establishing faith.

. I pray that:

My faith will increase continually…

My faith will increase continually…

My faith will increase continually,

…and I declare that I only grow from faith to faith. Let faith saturate these declarations. Let faith activate every declaration spoken by the Lord's decrees.

Let my belief in You, oh God, be credited to me as righteousness, through faith, in Jesus' Name. Amen.

# PRAY
# WAIT
# STAY
## 31 DAYS OF DECLARATIONS

# Day 16
# Healing

---

We have now completed the declarations of faith. I want us now to speak declarations of healing. I believe it is fitting, as we see in Scripture, where Jesus said more than once that 'faith' has made various biblical characters whole. I declare that the faith you have declared over the past three days will cause you to be whole as you pray and declare today.

## -Declarations-

Father, I know that if I cry for Your help, according to Psalm 30:2, You will hear and heal me. I pray for physical, mental, and emotional healing. I send this prayer to meet me in my future for where the enemy may want to inflict sickness. Let the words of this prayer and these declarations meet me in the future as a force of combat and fight against the enemy's plans in the MIGHTY Name of Jesus. Hallelujah!

Lord, I declare You to be the God who will heal all diseases, known and unknown, from me and my family, according to Psalm 103:3. You are the God who heals the brokenhearted and binds up their wounds, according to Psalm 147:3. I declare that wherever there is any residual hurt in me, You will take me through the necessary steps to receive emotional healing. Lord, help me to feel these emotions and not cover them up. Let them come to the surface with the intent of being dissolved and resolved, for You are the God concerned with the healing of the whole man. As I lay my hands on my head, let healing come to my mind and soul now, in Jesus' Name.

Everywhere I am weary, Lord, I ask that You give me strength - the strength spoken of in Isaiah 40:29. Lord, You declared in Jeremiah 30:17 that You will restore health and heal wounds. I thank You for restoring health for my family, myself, and those around me. I declare restored health and strength in Jesus' Name.

Father, Isaiah 53:5 says that You were wounded for my transgressions, crushed for my iniquities, the chastisement that brought us peace was upon You, and by Your stripes I am healed. I thank You for the representation of Your stripes upon me. I thank You for the healing that comes because of them. Lord, by this, I declare generational healing. If there can be generational curses, then there can be generational blessings.

I declare that all hereditary ailments are being eradicated from my bloodline now. Illnesses in the future, hear the words from my prophetic mouth and receive healing. I speak to the veins in my body right now, and I declare bloodline curses attached to illnesses are cut off from me now in the MIGHTY Name of Jesus.

It is so and shall not be otherwise in Jesus' Name. Amen.

# Day 17
## The Word and Study Life

---

The word of the Lord says in Romans 10:17 that faith comes by hearing and by hearing through the Word of Christ. We must listen and know the Good News of Christ Jesus to have faith. In essence, unless the Word is preached, there would be nothing to listen to because it is the Word of faith that brings salvation. As believers, we must know the Word of God. We must have a ready Word to speak on when the time comes to give an account of our faith and the hope that comes through salvation. Today, let us pray and make declarations concerning our Word and study life. As you pray today, take in your hand, prophetically, the Sword of the Spirit, which is the Word of God (See Ephesians 6:17). Let us declare.

## -Declarations-

Lord, I pray that I will always have a ready Word to share concerning the message of Jesus Christ. I declare that I will study to show myself approved unto God and rightly divide the Word according to 2 Timothy 2:15. I declare that I will eat of the Scroll daily just as You have commissioned Ezekiel in Ezekiel 3. I declare that I will walk, move, live, and breathe by Your Word.

According to the Scripture in Psalm 119:105, I declare that Your Word is a lamp unto my feet and a light unto my path leading me throughout this life. As I go throughout my day today, I declare that Your Word is so hidden in my heart, according to verse 11 of Psalm 119. It is so deeply rooted, so embedded in me, that I may not sin against You. Your Word declares in Luke 11:28 that those who hear and obey the Word of God are blessed and favoured. I declare that I am now, and always will be, obedient to Your Word, Lord. I declare that I am not just a hearer of Your Word but a doer, according to James 1:22. I am therefore blessed and favoured. Lord, I hate vain thoughts, but I do love Your Laws. You are my hiding place and shield: I hope in Your Word (Psalm 119:113-114, NIV). Romans 15:4 says everything written in the past was written to teach us so that we might have hope through the endurance taught in the Scriptures and the encouragement they provide. Lord, I hope in

Your Word. Guide me by Your Truth in Your Word (Psalm 25:5, AMP). Teach me, oh Lord, for You are the God of my salvation, and I wait on You daily.

Father, I know according to Scripture that every part of Your Word is genuine and has proven to be accurate, as was said in Proverbs 30:5. I thank You that the Scripture also says that You are a Shield to those who take refuge in You. I declare today that Your word, a lamp, and a light, is also a shield for me in Jesus' Name.

I declare that I will be prosperous and successful for I keep the Book of Your Law on my lips and meditate on it day and night according to Joshua 1:8.

Lord, I delight in Your Decrees; I will not neglect Your Word (Psalm 119:16, NIV). I declare that the Word dwells in me richly, as per Colossians 3:16. In Jesus' Name. Amen.

# Day 18
# The Hands and Feet

There is something of note to be said of the hands and feet in the Bible. The amplified version of Ephesians 2:10 informs us that "we are His workmanship [His own master work, a work of art], created in Christ Jesus [reborn from above—spiritually transformed, renewed, ready to be used] for good works, which God prepared [for us] beforehand [taking paths which He set], so that we would walk in them [living the good life which He prearranged and made ready for us]." This verse highlights that God has a preordained plan for us and the use of our skills. We are His hands and feet to carry out His good works here on earth. It is therefore fitting to speak on these two parts of the body and to make some declarations surrounding them for this New Year to inflict permanence for the rest of your days.

# -Declarations-

Lord, Your Word says, beautiful upon the mountains are the feet that carry the Good News (Isaiah 52:7, NIV). I declare today that my feet will carry the gospel of peace and the gospel of Your love far and wide.

I use the Blood as a weapon to cover my steps as I walk to and from each day. I declare that all my steps are ordered by the Lord (Psalm 37:23, KJV). Father, You provide a path for my feet so that my ankles do not give way (Psalm 18:36, NIV), so I thank You. I declare that I step with the Authority of Christ because Your Word says You give me authority over every territory where my feet are placed (Deuteronomy 11:24, NIV).

Now I declare that on the highways and byways, wherever I am sent for future days to come, I have full authority in Jesus' Name. I will give careful thought wherever I place my feet. I will be steadfast in all my ways. I will not turn to the right or the left and keep my feet from evil in Jesus' Name. Hallelujah!

Lord, regarding my hands, I pray that whatever I touch in Your Name is blessed. I declare that whatever I put my hands on will prosper in Jesus' Name (Deuteronomy 28:8, NIV). I pray and repent for everything contrary to You that my hand has ever touched or ever done.

Lord, I pray that You cleanse my hands from all evil deeds. Let not my hands be what cause me to be far from You. Lord, today I declare that my hands will be used only to do Your Will, to praise and to be lifted in worship to You. I declare that I will lift my hands in Your Name (Psalm 63:4, NIV) and as an offering (Psalm 141:2, NIV) in Jesus' Name.

I declare that my hands will do more significant works in Jesus' Name (John 14:12, NIV). I will lay my hands on the sick, and they will be healed (Mark 16:18, AMP); the sight will be restored to the blind through the works of my hands (Mark 8:22-26, AMP) in Jesus' Name.

I declare that my hands and feet are covered as I am the hands and feet of Jesus on the earth. Lord, I thank You for holding my hands throughout my journey in this life. I am comprehensively covered in the firm Name of Jesus (Isaiah 51:16, AMP). Amen.

# Day 19
## Destiny

---

Lord, today I make declarations regarding my destiny, and I declare that my destiny is secured in You. I thank You that my destiny is secure in You (Ephesians 1:11, NIV). Lord, You said that before I was born from my mother's womb, You gave me my destiny that I would fulfill the plan and purpose You have for me in Your heart. I pray and come against any plan, plot, or evil scheme of the enemy to derail me. As I have previously declared, I declare that my steps are ordered. I stand today flat-footed and secured in God's Will and divine plan for my life. I declare aloud that my future is secured in Christ. Today, I consciously decide to bless the Lord all my days. I declare that His praise will forever be on my lips (Psalm 34:1, NIV). It is my destiny to praise the Lord, for it is You, God, that has made me, and I was not made by myself (Psalm 100:3, AMP), so, I will praise You. It is not Your Will that I may perish (2 Peter 3:9, KJV), and so I praise You. You said that You would give me the good desires of my heart (Psalm 37:4, NIV), so I praise You. You said

You would rebuke the devourer for my sake (Malachi 3:11, KJV), so Lord, I praise You. Hallelujah!

Right now, I come against every spirit of distraction that would like to occupy my time in place of what God ordains me to do. I rebuke the distractions of social media, the distractions that come through the affairs of men, my work life, and anything that would want to make itself an idol in my life to distract me from my purpose. Lord, I yield the 'high things' in my life and declare they are now made low in Jesus' Name.

I declare that I will fulfill what I have been placed here on earth to do, and nothing by any means shall distract me from doing so in time and season. Hallelujah! Lord, I declare just like the sons of Issachar that I will operate in my correct time and season. In this New Year, Lord, I will know Your Will for the rest of my days. I will know the cause You have for me in every place that I will set my foot.

I declare that at every time and in every season, even throughout this very year, I will, I must, I shall do what You have called me to. I will operate at my place of influence as You have called me to be influential as a child of God in Jesus' Name. Amen.

# Day 20
# Against Lack and Scarcity

Lord, today, as I come before You, I pray concerning lack and scarcity. Lord, You said in Your Word that no good thing will be withheld from them that walk uprightly (Psalm 84:11, AMP). I declare that I am Your child; search my heart, Lord, and see that I walk uprightly. I rebuke and send the Fire of the Holy Ghost to the spirit of lack in the Name of Jesus. I rip off the garment of lack from my life and from anything and anyone that lack is attached to. I declare you, lack, be moved like the mountain you think you are. Be moved now! You, the spirit of lack, will no longer plague my life in Jesus' Name.

I declare that I am prosperous in all my ways and doing (Psalm 20:4, NIV). No longer will financial lack be associated with me. The Word of the Lord in Ecclesiastes 10:19 says that money answers all things. By the Lord's Word, I declare that money now answers for me. I declare that money will answer for me in the Mighty Name of Jesus. In every area of my life that money is lacking, I call on you prophetically by the Word of the Lord, and I command money to answer for me now! By force, by favour, and by fire, answer now! Lack and scarcity will not be my portion. You will not be the portion over my home in Jesus' Name. I send these declarations to my fridge and cupboard. I speak to the spirit of lack over my wallet/purse, and command you to go! You will not meet me in the future! Flee to dry and desolate places in the Name of Jesus. Hallelujah!

You said You would rebuke the devourer for my sake, so, Lord, I thank You! Thank You for rebuking the devourer on my behalf. I thank You that You said that You will pour me out a blessing that I have no room to receive (Malachi 3:10, AMP). I declare today that wealth, as by Your Word, is stored up for me (Proverbs 13:22, NIV). I thank You that wealth is attached to my name. I thank You, Lord, for Your promises for me are yes and amen (2 Corinthians 1:20, AMP), so, for every whisper of the enemy concerning the things I do not yet have and for the things my eyes are not able to see, I thank You that I have already received them by the Spirit of the Lord. I thank You that I have a Godly inheritance stored up for me in the Name of Jesus. I thank You that for whatever the enemy says no to, I am reminded of Your yes.

Abba, I bless You, honour You, and thank You for Your goodness and love. I thank You that lack and scarcity are now far from me and far from those attached to me in the Name of Jesus. Amen.

# Day 21
## Worship

---

There is a song written by Pastor Dean Smith that has the lines, "Even in trouble, You are still great. Forever and always still the same. When oppositions rise, we will call on the Name that demons fear." That line gets me every time I listen to or sing that song. What a God, that even in trouble, nothing about Him changes! He is still the same God. The One who is a very present help (Psalm 46:1, KJV). This is the God we praise, which is why I want us to make declarations concerning worship. It does not matter what we face in this life, God is still who He said He would be. Our circumstance does not question His character, and for this cause, I want us to make some declarations to praise Him despite the bad times we may encounter. Hallelujah! Let's pray.

## -Declarations-

Lord, today I thank You. I declare that I will always bless You, and Your praise will forever be on my lips (Psalm 34:1, NIV). I will rise to bless You (Psalm 92:2, AMP), and my circumstances will not dictate my praise. Hallelujah! I declare Your Word, as stated in 1 Chronicles 16:23-34 that I will sing of Your love forever. I will proclaim Your saving power to all the earth. I will declare Your glory among the nations, Your marvelous deeds among all people. For great are You LORD and most worthy of praise; You are to be feared above all gods. Hallelujah! Lord, I will worship You in the beauty of Your holiness.

Father, with every breath within me, I will praise You (Psalm 150:6, NIV). I will praise You when I am happy and through my sad times. I will praise even through any ailment because I know that the stripes of Your Son have already healed me. You are the God who rescues the life of the needy from the hands of the wicked (Jeremiah

20:13, NIV), so I praise You.

Lord, may it not be said that I come near to You with my mouth and honour You with my lips, but my heart is far from You (Isaiah 29:13, AMP). I declare that my worship is not based merely on the human rules I have been taught. I declare that

I will give You the glory that is due to Your Name (Psalm 29:2, KJV) in Jesus' Name. Amen.

# Day 22
## A Vow to Praise

I have shared the story many times on multiple platforms of how the Lord truly set me up to be the worshipper that I am. Many years ago, I was leading worship in church, and the Lord caused me to stray away from my set list to sing the song "Praise is what I do" by William Murphy. He kept on having me emphasize the lines, "I vow to praise You through the good and the bad. I'll praise You, whether happy or sad. I'll praise You in all I go through because praise is what I do." I will never forget standing on that stage and feeling so pressed to make that vow to the Lord. I even asked the congregation to make the vow, not knowing how much it would mean for me. Wow! Since then, I have been through some of the most troubling situations that would cause anyone to question God, to want to give up on Him, and even to lose their sanity (which I almost did, but that is a story for another book *winks*). Today, I want us to make that vow to praise Him.

I will never forget the time that I ended up homeless, sleeping on the cold floor of a friend's house with just a blanket to cover the floor. With tears running down my face, I rocked from side to side while singing that very song - "I vow to praise You..." Will you make this vow with me today? Let's pray.

## -Declarations-

Lord, today I genuinely make a vow to praise You. Through any situation, Lord, I will praise You. Father, with tears streaming down my face, I will praise You. When my soul is cast down, I will hope in You and praise You. When I receive the most devastating news, Lord, I will praise You. Father, when I receive victory over a thing I have been praying for, I will not forget to praise You.

Lord, help me to remember this vow that I am making today because I know I am human and will forget.

Lord, You said in Isaiah 57:15 that You dwell on the high and holy place, but also with the contrite and humble spirit. You said that You revive the spirit of the humble and those that are contrite.

Lord, that is why I praise You. I will praise You for reviving my spirit when I am down. Glory to Your Name!

I will praise You, according to Psalm 30:1-4. Lord, You lifted me out of the depths and did not let my enemies rejoice over me. Each time I have called for Your help, You have done a continuous work of healing in me. You have kept me alive so that I would not go down to the grave. Hallelujah! Father, Your love is better than life; I declare that my lips will glorify and praise You as long as I live, as in Psalm 63:3-4.

Everything that is within me will PRAISE YOU. In Jesus' Name. Amen.

# Day 23
## Seek the Lord

---

There is something so refreshing about the Presence of God. The newness and revival from His holy and sweet Spirit is so refreshing. Praising God brings comity, calm, stillness, and peace. It is vital to our walk as believers to dwell in His presence. How do we know His presence? When we seek Him, we will find Him, but it is only AFTER we have searched with *all* of our hearts (Jeremiah 29:13, NIV). Today, I want us to declare that we will seek the Lord and go deeper in this seek. Let us pray.

## -Declarations-

Lord, today I come before You and long for Your presence. I know that in Your presence, there is fullness of joy. I thank You for the joy that comes from Your presence. Thank you also for the peace, hope, and pleasures always. Lord, You make known the path of life (Psalm 16:11, AMP). I declare that as I seek after You, I will find You. I declare that I will search for You with all my heart. Your Word says, in Matthew 5:8, that the pure in heart shall see God. I ask that You clean my hands and purify my heart so that I will find You, upon my declaration of seeking to see You. Hallelujah!

Lord, I thank You for Your presence, which can go with me to give me rest (Exodus 33:14, NIV). I thank You for the times of refreshing that come from being in Your presence (Acts 3:19, NIV). One thing I have asked of the LORD [and] that I will seek after that I may dwell in the house of the LORD all the days of my life, to gaze upon the beauty of the LORD and to inquire in his temple (Psalm 27:4, NIV). Hallelujah!

May Your glory surround me. May I dwell in the most holy of holies. Lord, may I experience singing and dancing with Your holy angels. May the more I seek You, the more I *want* to seek You. Lord, may I go deeper and never be deep enough. In Jesus' Name, I pray, Amen.

# Day 24
## Surrender

Sometimes, we make hasty decisions in our Christian walk. We decide on things, but we do not consult the Lord. We have made declarations on wisdom, so that is not what we will declare here today. Today, I want us to pray concerning our level of surrender. I am unsure if there is a specific flow you might be looking for the book to go in (I thought I would have had one), but God would have it that I write as He leads and *only* how He leads. Yesterday, I wrote about the Presence of God, and while writing, I heard the word "surrender." I have come to understand that to indeed dwell in the Presence of God, we must surrender our will to His. He has to have all our attention for us to see Him. Romans 12:2 says that we are to be transformed and progressively changed by renewing our minds as we mature spiritually. It says that we are to focus on Godly values; by this, there is no room for our earthly quarrels. The Scripture also goes further to say that when our minds are transformed, we will be able to know what the Will of God is for ourselves. Do we know what the Will of God is? Do we want to know and be transformed? Believers, if we have not yet surrendered, it is time to surrender all. Let us pray.

## -Declarations-

Father, as I come before You, I place my will at Your feet. I lay my human understanding down before You. I place my future and all of my plans, and I say take all of it and give me all of You. Lord, I surrender all to You. I lay my desires at the altar and ask that You be the dominant force surrounding my life. I pray today, and I fully surrender my heart to You. It does not make sense to pray for anything that comes from You without a surrendered life. I cannot truly worship You if I am not fully surrendered.

Therefore, Lord, I repent for everything I have made an idol over You that has hindered my worship, my time in the Word, and my time in prayer. Father, I pray and declare that I will resist the devil and no longer succumb to the temptations he brings because I know that if I resist him, according to James 4:7, he will flee. I, therefore, fully submit myself to You. Jesus, you said that if I am to come after You, I must deny myself, then take up my cross and follow You. According to Luke 9:23, I will take up my cross daily and follow You. According to Galatians 2:20, I declare that I have been crucified with Christ. Father, it is no longer I who live but You who live within me.

I pray that I will walk, live, and move in Your Word from a fully surrendered life. Take away my earthly desires completely. The desire for social media and desires to be validated by men. In my job and daily life, I surrender everything. I ask that You make me new by this surrender.

I declare that I will first seek the Kingdom of God and all His righteousness because I know that by this, all things will be added unto me according to Matthew 6:33. In Jesus' Name.

---

*Focus on Godly values; by this, there is no room for our earthly quarrels.*

---

# Day 25
# Wage a Good War

---

Your life and destiny are essential to God. A generation of no-nonsense people are rising, waging a good war against the enemy. After we have done all the declarations throughout the days in this book, the enemy will want to find ways to retaliate and raise his ugly head. I want us to wage a good war for the next seven days. To pray against any opposition that may arise because of the declarations made. Let's wage war and settle the matter for our lives until the end of this book in Jesus' Name.

## -Declarations-

Father, in the Name of Jesus, I pray against the enemy's plot, plan, and evil scheme to derail me this season. I declare that the Word of God settles my days, life, and entire destiny in Jesus' name. Even after I have made these many days of declarations, the matter concerning all the declarations by the Lord's decrees is settled. The matter is settled. Everything declared IS SO and shall not be otherwise in Jesus' MIGHTY Name.

I declare that every word spoken has been established in the heavens (Psalm 119:89). I do not pray in vain. I did not receive this book in vain. My declarations will fall on fertile soil, and I declare a blossoming by the roots in the realm of the Spirit now.

I speak a divine alignment over my life for the rest of my days, in Jesus' Name.

# Day 26
# No Evil Befalls Me

---

L ord, today I pray, and I declare that no evil befalls me, nor will any plague come near me (Psalm 91:10, AMP). I stand to declare, according to Your Word, that I shall not die, but live to declare the works of the Lord until the end of my days (Psalm 118:17, KJV). I declare that the Blood writes for me and blots out every handwriting that seeks to contend with these declarations even as days have passed (Colossians 2:14, KJV). I declare that these declarations redeem me, renew me, and revive me.

Every retaliating spirit set to oppose the declarations made, I command you to be consumed by the Fire of the Almighty God. Every monitoring spirit that is sent to monitor my words, so they do not come to pass, I declare you to be made desolate now. I rebuke you by the Blood and Fire of the GREAT and TERRIBLE God.

I reiterate that my life is firmly fitted in the Hands of God, and the enemy cannot thwart the Will of God for me in Jesus' Name.

# Day 27
# Redemption Through
# the Blood

---

L ord, today I thank You that it is not by my might nor by my power, but by Your Spirit that I am victorious (Zechariah 4:6, KJV). I declare aloud today as a reminder to the enemy that I have redemption by and through Your Blood (Hebrews 9:12, NIV). I declare that it is the Blood of Jesus that speaks for me (Hebrews 12:24, NIV). It is the Blood that covers me and cries out on my behalf. The enemy has no power over me because I have security in the Blood. Hallelujah!

Now, I thank God, who gives me victory and causes me to triumph. (1 Corinthians 15:57, KJV)

I declare that the faithful Lord will strengthen me and protect me from the evil one. (2 Thessalonians 3:3, NIV) I declare that I have strength and am protected from the evil one in Jesus' Name. I declare that I have the power and the authority to tread, so right now, I tread prophetically, upon every serpent and scorpion, and over all the power of the enemy, and nothing shall, by any means, hurt me (Luke 10:19, NIV) in Jesus' Name. Amen

# Day 28
# Holding No Hostage

Father, today I pray to the God who will cause the enemies that rise against me to be defeated before me. I pray to God that He will cause those who come against me to flee in several, different ways right before my eyes. (Deuteronomy 28:7, NIV) I recognize You, Lord, as this God today. The One who will not let the enemy laugh and say, "Aha aha! Our eyes have seen it." (Psalm 35:21, AMP) I thank You for being that God—the One who is not slack concerning His promises.

I declare that there will never be a season of my life in which the enemy will have an opportunity to laugh. Let the enemy choke at the very thought of laughter. Let every demonic entity that sets its mouth to speak against me choke, vomit, and die in their blood. Lord, anything that is in opposition to what You said and who You are is in rebellion and is therefore considered a witch (1 Samuel 15:23, KJV). I suffer not a witch to live (Exodus 22:18, KJV). This I pray Mighty God - any witch assigned to my life to derail me or any witch assigned for me not to fulfill my purpose, by the Will and Word of God, their evil words and weapons will not prosper in Jesus' Name (Isaiah 54:17, NIV).

I hold no hostage to things that would applaud at my downfall. I declare that every pit dug by the enemy for me to fall in, those who dug it will fall in the same pit first, in Jesus' Name (Psalm 7:15, KJV). It is so and shall not be otherwise in Jesus' Name.

# Day 29
# The Lord Fights for Me

I declare that every word I utter is laced with the Fire of the Almighty God. My words are like a sword cutting through every demonic enchantment in the Name of Jesus.

I say with all my might that I, _____, do not fear, for the Lord my God fights for me. (Deuteronomy 3:22, AMP)

Surely! If God is for me, WHO CAN BE AGAINST ME? WHO? (Romans 8:31, KJV)

Will I not run through a troop and leap over walls? (Psalm 18:29, KJV) Will I not break barriers in the Name of the Lord? I declare that it is so! Hallelujah!

Through You, Lord, I will push back my adversaries. In the Name of Jesus, I will trample those who rise against me. (Psalm 44:5, NIV) You, Lord, have subdued, under my feet, those who have revolted against me. (Psalm 18:39, AMP)

I declare that I will not be afraid or discouraged because of what may come against me. I declare that the battle is not mine, but the Lord's in Jesus' Name. Amen. (2 Chronicles 20:15, NIV)

# Day 30
## The Settlement

Father, by Your Power and in Your Name, I pray that the words spoken from this book are gone before me as a mighty force.

The enemy will not be able to stop or block what these declarations, by the decrees of the Lord, are set out to accomplish.

I have now been reminded of who I am in Christ, and I declare that this memory will never depart from me, nor will His Words depart from my mouth. My life is settled. His Will for me is settled. I am settled. All have been settled in the Strong and Mighty Name of Jesus.

Who can stand against the Lord and win? None! I declare that with Christ living in me, none can stand; no power in hell will be able to stand against me in the Name of Jesus. Amen.

# Day 31
# Sealed

---

Lord, today, on the last day of declarations, I seal every word declared by the Blood and under the Blood. I declare complete Blood coverage in the Name of Jesus. Right now, I reinstall the whole Armour of God over my life to guard against every attack that comes from the enemy.

I put on the Belt of Truth that will dispel any lie spoken from the mouth of the accuser.

I reinstall the Breastplate of Righteousness to protect my heart from temptations I may face. It also protects Your Word hidden in my heart, that I may not sin against You, Lord.

I reinstall the Gospel of Peace on my feet. I declare that light will permeate with every step I take from this day forth. I walk covered, in freedom, and with peace in every step in the Name of Jesus. Lord, I will take Your light wherever I am sent, and it will shine so brightly that others seated in Heaven will see and want to glorify You.

I reposition the Shield of Faith in my hand that will cover me from every fiery dart sent my way.

I reinstall the Helmet of Salvation to keep my mind covered and at peace.

I hold firmly in my hand the Sword of the Spirit, which is Your Word, as an offensive weapon against the enemy.

Complete coverage will be my portion for the rest of my days in Jesus' Name. Amen.

# CONCLUSION

---

Now that you have done your declarations, how do you feel?

A few pages have been placed at the end for you to document your own experience and keep a record of your encounters throughout these past 31 days.

My prayer is that this book has truly blessed you. I pray that as you have declared and prayed, you will sit at the feet of your Father and wait to see the manifestations of these declarations. After the testimonies come, may you stay at His feet and make those feet your permanent residence...Oh, to dwell.

Believers, my heart desires that you will be transformed by the reading of this book. Thank you for journeying through these 31 days.

May your posture ever be to...
***Pray. Wait. Stay.***

# PRAY WAIT STAY

## 31 DAYS OF DECLARATIONS

# Personal Declarations
# and Testimonies

_____

_____

_____

_____

_____

_____

_____

_____

_____

_____

_____

_____

_____

_____

_____

_____

_____

_____

_____

_____

_____

_____

# ABOUT THE AUTHOR

Lashawn Wilson is a Jamaican Gospel Minister, singer, songwriter, recording gospel artiste, conference host, mentor, and author. Affectionately known as 'Psalmist Lashawn,' she is widely recognized for her ability to shift atmospheres and invoke a sense of glory in her ministry across the island of Jamaica.

An intercessor at heart, Lashawn has been known to petition God's Throne on behalf of His people, and He often gives her specific spiritual insights in her times of crying out to Him.

She is the founder and visionary behind the Weeping, Wailing, Worshipping Women's Conference - an event designed to empower women to fearlessly use their weeping, wailing and worship as a weapon. She is also the founder and visionary behind Glory in The Morning: A Sunrise Worship Experience - an event geared at truly understanding the Glory of God and dwelling in His presence. Lashawn firmly believes that those who grasp the potency of their worship, hold tremendous power.

One of her cherished scriptures is John 4:23: 'But the hour is coming, and now is, when the true worshipers will worship the Father in spirit and truth, for such the Father seeks to worship Him.'

www.ingramcontent.com/pod-product-compliance
Lightning Source LLC
LaVergne TN
LVHW051250080426
835513LV00016B/1844